CW00742847

'The inspiringly titled **Fruitful Tho**
us gingerfish, blissful summer breezes, p
blackness, raindrop memories, evil little
and pictures which will kick us all back in touch with our adolescent
selves.'

Jan Patience, arts journalist, *The Herald*

'The honesty and directness of the writers' approach gave their
work real emotional power.'

Anne Donovan, author of *Buddha Da*

'The wild horses shown and written about here won't be needed
to drag readers of all ages towards this excellent book (and series).
To the marvellous bestiary, is added a series of poetic contemplations,
taking in states of mind, emotions and concepts such as love and anger.
Work on that abstract scale is hard to bring off. All the more reason to
salute these young writers and artists. From the masterly poems and
prints about siblings, parents and other relatives, one can draw mostly
reassuring conclusions about family life in this part of Scotland.
Peruse. And use!'

Donny O'Rourke, poet, journalist, broadcaster

'Adolescence is a universal experience, none of us escape it.
Willie Rodger, Liz Lochhead and the writers and illustrators of this
collection have compiled a compelling catalogue of the observations,
joys, miseries, anxieties and expectations inherent in one of life's most
unsettling milestones. Congratulations!'

Peter McCormack, curator, Auld Kirk Museum

'Visual imagery brilliantly captured – "purple and glittery"!
These pupils will surely remember their experience of working with
Willie Rodger and Liz Lochead.'

Jane Cameron, curator, University of Stirling

# Fruitful Thoughts of Adolescents

# Fruitful Thoughts of Adolescents

**St Ninian's High School**

Media Matters
Education Consultancy Ltd.

**A Media Matters Book**

First published in 2010 by
Media Matters Education Consultancy Ltd
104 Barscube Terrace
Paisley
PA2 6XH
www.mediamatters.co.uk

ISBN 978-1-907693-03-8

Front Cover: © Shannon Kerr
Back Cover: © Gillian Smyth

Printed in the Great Britain by Lightning Source UK Ltd

Published by Media Matters Education Consultancy Ltd
in association with East Dunbartonshire Council.

sustainable thriving achieving

**East Dunbartonshire Council**

www.eastdunbarton.gov.uk

For Ms Harper - the memory lives on  x
And for all those who were harmed in the making of this book

The creation, marketing and selling of this book is being run as a
social enterprise with net profits being donated to the
**Scottish Catholic International Aid Fund (SCIAF).**

# PREFACE

How often as a pupil were you given a task which began "Imagine that you have to------" and then ordered to produce a piece for a magazine or a product for a client?

Well, these lucky S3 pupils were given the opportunity to construct a live product for commercial sale and how wonderfully well they have risen to the task! This anthology is well worthy of its place on retail booksellers' shelves. The pupil-generated content and illustrations fully justify the professional finish accorded by the layout.

As with most things in education, however, the benefits lie as much in the processes undertaken as in the artefact produced. Our young people have thrived in an atmosphere of cooperation while experiencing some of the pitfalls of creative tension and business relationships to produce this outstanding work – joined up learning in every sense of the term.

Congratulations to them, their teachers and the external consultants involved.

*Paul McLaughlin*
Headteacher
May 2010

# CONTENTS

# PART II

# PART III

# APPENDICES

# LINO-CUTS

# LINO-CUTS

*Willie Rodger, RSA*

# FOREWORD

BY LIZ LOCHHEAD

When working with East Dunbartonshire secondary schools last Autumn on my part of this creative writing and making-of-a-book initiative -- via GLOW, the ground-breaking, Scotland-wide, first national intranet for Education, no less! -- I kept thinking of my friend Adrian Mitchell, the poet, who died just over a year ago. Adrian would have loved this book. He loved going in to schools and sharing his poems with pupils, and he loved encouraging and helping pupils to write their own -- and he used to put at the start of all his books that none of the poems in it were to be used for any Examination Purposes whatsoever!

Here is an extract from something he wrote about the point of poetry, and of poets:

*It is the job of poets to arouse all those parts of the imagination which are asleep or numb. To feed the imagination, to extend the imagination. To use the imagination, to defend the imagination. To explore the imagination. To risk drowning in the imagination.*

*To be fools. To be glad when they are called fools. To be reminders of doom when they are asked for jokes. To be relentless comedians when asked to be serious.*

*To be jugglers of images, verbal clowns......*

*To overcome their own fears. To show people how fears can be overcome, slowly, one by one.*

*To celebrate life. To attack the enemies of life...*

13

*Foreword: Liz Lochhead*

Waking up our own imaginations is important work. Easy when we realise that our five sound senses (if we are lucky enough to have all five of them) and the real world around us, and our memory, and the simple truth (which is rarely simple) and the plain ordinary words we use every day (better, far better, than any of those swallowed-a-dictionary ones) are all we need.

And a pencil or a biro and a jotter.

Oh, the marvels of computers, and webcams – and GLOW, when it was up and working... Now, I'm far less technology-literate than most of the pupils I met, but I can say it was truly amazing to go into nine classes simultaneously and for us to do a 'creative writing workshop' in real time together. Later on, it was even better to go (webcam again) into one class at a time and talk face-to-face with pupils about the work they had posted each week. It was great, from the computer on my desktop at home, to go into the pages and read the drafts and rewrites as they got posted – and, best of all, explore the feedback (mostly praise, but lots of friendly and very constructive criticism too!) that these young poets were getting, not only from their own classmates, but also, more and more as we got further into it, from pupils -- and teachers -- in other schools. Colleagues they had only met in this virtual environment. Communication though! Real communication.

The teachers worked incredibly hard on this. The pupils too, who were often spoilt for choice about what piece or pieces to put into the book, they had achieved so much - usually three poems which had gone through several drafts. I hope they are all as proud and pleased to be in print here as they ought to be.

From the moment you open *Fruitful Thoughts of Adolescents* from St. Ninian's, perhaps dipping in and out of its treasures at random, as this lucky-bag of an anthology invites you to do, you'll be in a world that's in turn, thoughtful, revealing, personal, vivid, and often very witty. See how one poet dramatises, beautifully, in *The Standoff* the progress of an argument as it flares and ebbs, and how strong the linoprint that accompanies it; how another double-page spread celebrates a life-long friendship with a piece on each page from the point of view of each of its participants; how *Granny June* 'makes the greatest chips' – because it's always by celebrating the specific that a character is made to live and breathe; how another poet, writing in the voice of a pen, notes: *'I mean so much more than e-mail or text/ my ink comes straight from the heart'*; how another, writing about *Pigeons* says: *as they fly by you can taste the city/ – a standing ovation as their wings flap'*; yet another, writing about My Little Brother with his *'monkey-like face'*, then goes all the way with his own illustration. Very Cheeky!

My friend Willie Rodger, the great printmaker and artist, once again via GLOW, did workshops on both lino-cutting and illustration – how important to get to the essence of something, how vital to be simple, do just one idea, strong and clear. The poets, as they handed over their work to their partner in the Art Class, would, I know, have recognised this paring-down process.

This book, I'm sure you'll agree, would be so much less without its illustrations. They are strong, subtle, funny, bold, beautiful. There is a real dialogue between the words and the pictures. (The poem *Destruction* made doubly dynamic by the knock-out energy of the print of the same name by its side; that *My Little Sister* is evil... But brilliant! Etc, etc..)

The medium of the lino-print, the black ink on the white page, grants a unity to an astonishing range of styles and images. All independent of, but complementing, the words that inspired them.

As I write this foreword, feeling excited as I look, online once again, at the projected design and lay-out of this very volume which you now hold in your hand, I realise I have already learned a lot, second-hand, from this enterprise the Business Education pupils are now embarked upon, about the production of, and distribution of, books. (And I thought I was a professional as well!)

The decisions made – after all the passionate arguments -- about the best choice of title, which charity ought to benefit, the design of the cover, how to price it, the publicity for and the marketing of it, have all required a lot more of that communication between different authors, artists, individuals, classes and disciplines in the school. More of that wonderful thing the whole world needs more of: Joined-Up Learning.

*Liz Lochhead March 2010*

# PART I

# Frazer

The jingle of its collar
Makes you turn round and see
It sprawled across your driveway
Or peeking out from under the car

Its beady eyes stare at you
And force you to quickly turn away
Its sharp claws move slowly across the ground
As it flashes its pointed teeth

*Rachael McKay*

*Christopher Coyle*

# Nemo

It's not a 'goldfish': it's a gingerfish.

It's not 'scaly' or 'wet': it's slimy.

It gets bullied. It's boring.  It's pointless.

Its attempts to befriend others fail - no wonder.

Some may try to jazz it up by pretending it's purple and glittery.

But pretending isn't real - pretending

is pretend.

Who would even bother to try to find Nemo?

*Sara Maxwell*

*Christopher Coyle*

# Pigeons

As they fly by, you can taste the city -
A standing ovation as their wings flap.
They walk the streets like a gang,
prowling the streets since streets began.
They coo all day and even at night
and then annoy the people down below.
They cause a mess and make people sick.
Their claws on the ground go clickety click.
Flying rats, flying vermin
I just call them the
Neighbourhood pigeons

*Gregory Fulton*

Joseph McPhee

22

# A Drowned Squirrel

I was approaching the dam at around noon.
I was in a happy mood and I was feeling fresh!
A small, stout, grumpy looking man came into view.
We approached him inquiring about his present activities.
He replied, that he was doing his job, in a stern tone;
I could smell the dampness of the man's unwashed uniform!
There were dark, moist circles of sweat beneath his underarms;
their scent lingered in my nostrils.
He was holding a metal basket with a long pole attached.
My friend immediately blurted out "There're bubbles."
He replied "There aren't anymore!"
My heart skipped a beat as I glared down at the contents at the cage.
Three lifeless squirrels lay
dead!

*Shannon Kerr*

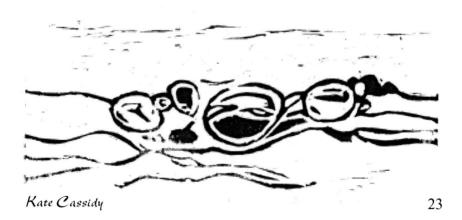

*Kate Cassidy*

24

Shannon Kerr

# Horse

As he gallops through the moors
Arching his neck and snorting too
His tail is swishing side to side.
The mighty stallion runs free with pride.

He's gliding through the springtime breeze.
The long fresh grass, sweeps his knees.
His smooth silk coat gleams in the sunlight.
The people gaze in awe at this beautiful sight.

Children and adults, stop and stare
As this beautiful beast poses with flare.
He jumps and rears, impressing his audience.
He has not even been trained with any obedience.

As it gets dark, he turns around.
He gallops away as the sun goes down.
The sound of his hoofs are heard in the night.
The stallion is finally out of sight.

*Charlotte Gillan*

# The Horse

The swish of its tail slicing through the icy cold air
The click of its hooves against the frozen ground
The mid-morning sun beats down upon its slick black coat
The cool winter breeze whips through its thick main

*Kate Cassidy*

*Melissa Clarke*

# My Neighbour's Dog

Under the tree I can see
My neighbour's dog tied.
I wonder what he has done.
Their dog is called 'Puppy'.
He's quite small, short and skinny.
Nobody appreciates him, except his owners.
He often gets into fights
And bites people.
He is also vicious and ugly.
His back knees are locked
So he walks funny
But when he chases you
Things are definitely going to get scary.

*Kevin Romero*

*Roxann Ingleby*

# PART II

Caillan Gallacher

# Bliss

I am a calm summer breeze, tickling your skin,
the warm sand beneath your toes,
that fuzzy feeling when the plane climbs high above the clouds.
I tell you to stop,
lie down,
and appreciate me while I'm here.
I'm the times that have become memories,
with the people you want to stay with, forever.
I am laughing 'til your tummy hurts,
I smell like coconut suntan lotion,
and the sea rushing, to and fro.
I am waiting for Santa on Christmas eve,
Waking up with a smile,
The safe feeling of knowing someone loves you,
Hot chocolate, calming, warming.
I am hearing the blistering gales
and pelting rain tap against the window,
when you know you dont't have to get out of bed.
I will make you smile, and you won't even care if your nose crinkles.
I am bliss, the closest thing to heaven you will encounter.

*Ciara McShane*

# Who Am I?

I am what's in your heart
An emotion, taken for granted
I am the colour red
Warm, passionate
I am the butterflies in your stomach
When you see that special someone
I am the sound of laughter
No fear is in my presence
I am the smell of roses
The sweet aroma of friendship
I am the season summer
The freedom that it brings
Most of all, I am a part of you
Your imagination is my guide
Who am I?
I am Love

*Catriona McNicoll*

Adele Ferns

# Love

I am a group of teenagers flirtatiously laughing.
I am the red sky at night when the sun is almost set.
I am the smell of roses freshly planted.
I am the taste of peppermint chewing gum, minty fresh.
I am a gentle touch from a caring mother

*Paula Carrigan*

Gillian Smyth

# Love

I can be anything
I can be anywhere
I can be anyone
I am like a blank canvas
Like a white shawl
enveloping a baby.
I am the sweetness,
not the bitterness
I am the water lapping over the sand
I am unconditional and unwanting

I am the sun
though some say I am the thunder
Unwanting or unwanted?
Like a thousand hugs or a thousand knives?
Am I the lie that draws a smile or the truth that draws a tear?

I am Love

*Louise Tonner*

Rebecca McCafferty

## Love

I am a heartbeat - constant.

I am a red sky at night as the sun sets - beautiful.

I am the saying you love to hear from that special person - meaningful.

I am red - passionate.

I am soft, warm, and yummy - everything.

I am love - perfection.

*Ciatlin Hughes*

# Red Ribbon

Floating in the air
across the cloudless blue sky,
swaying in the breeze.
Showing off its flawless beauty.
The silk red ribbon.
Soft and comforting,
fell a thousand feet down.
Dancing gracefully.
My heart broke in two.
Red fabric split down the middle,
separated from myself,
lost in deep despair.
I ran across the footpath
searching for a part of me that was no where to be seen.
Red,
struck through my heart with a dagger.
Everything.
Everyone.
Disappeared.
I slowly touched the ground,
into the everlasting darkness.

*Rebecca McCafferty*

Yasmin Blake

Caillan Gallacher

# Our Land

Elated
As I taste those peppermint kisses
Lingering on my lips

My vision obscured
As we run hand in hand, in the rain
Whilst the sun shines through the trees
As we run in a land
Of Euphoria

Dusk greets us
Hand in hand
In our land, of Euphoria

We are alone, in our land
It's our land: it's our world
Where we are
Eternally blissful

In our arms
Is our eternal
Euphoria

*Francine McQuade*

# Excitement

Excitement is:
the first time a child sees snow
with a sound of laughter and squeals
its the smell of sweets
with a taste of chocolate
Excitement is:
the feeling of fur
with a colour of orange
its wearing bright summer clothes
because it's a bright, warm, summer's day.

*Clare Fitzpatrick*

*Corrine Cairney*

# Totoro </3

Standing in the pouring rain,
he nervously adjusts his fringe.
He was obnoxious of her feelings
as his hoodie reflected the stars.

She stood solid, statuesque,
But inside she was crumbling, crying, dying.
As she turned to walk away
a tear escaped her eye.
It landed in a puddle, rippling, crippling.
She saw him skate away, not looking back.

It follows us everywhere
looking for a chance to jump in,
losing friends, losing status.
A cold, harsh slap -
rejection.

The repetitive blackness that he imprinted on her brain
was just like the skinny jeans imprinted on his frame.

*Eve Mcneill*

# Anger

Sirens.
The high-pitched sound screams in your ears
The flash of light sharply blinding your vision
The smell of smoke filling your nostrils,
till you can take no more.

It fills up inside you
You must let it out
Thunder rumbling like a heart beating,
but more.

Burnt toast fills your tastebuds
Black and deep red lights flash through your brain
Like a bull, thundering towards a matador.

It's in control.
It's taking over.
You can't hold it in much longer.
It's anger.

*Charlotte Gillan*

# Fear!!

Silence?
Grey?
Then a thunder roar.

Dampness?
Hide.
Now a lightning strike.

A hoody?
Shaking?
Screams!

Cold?
Blood?
Is someone there?????

*Kerry Thompson*

*Ebony Lynch*

# Destruction

Stinging rain lashes at a laughing figure
Standing amidst a sea of the dead
A manic grin graces its face
Its hands are stained with darkening red

The air feels like steel and madness and death
Eyes are clouded with hazy crimson mist
Senses are panicked, disorientated and above all scared
As the figure is filled with morbid joy

Others look at the scene of horror
Some laughing, some crying, some nodding
Some turn away - unable to act -
Hoping it won't come their way
As destruction laughs the night away

*Catherine Fodey*

Rachael Holmes

48

# Loss

You strike through my heart like a gust of wind
stealing the leaves from a tree.
Heartbreak is unbearable.

You destroy anything that makes me happy.
A wild storm cannot match your destruction.
You are always on my mind.

You paint everything that is good in the world black.
Taking over my life.
I hear crying, wailing, sobbing.

You torment me like a baby crying, high-pitched and in pain.
I want to correct the problem but I don't know where to start.
You make me helpless.

It becomes too much to bear.
The tears begin to fall.
The pain slowly but surely takes over.
Then decreases.
I am free.

*Ailidh O'Brien*

# Time

Always moving, it never stops.

The never ending pictures of life passing by.

The clock-like sound of the rain on the roof,

It's as though for every raindrop a new memory is made.

But it's only the sweet raindrop memories that are kept forever.

The roof prevents the sour ones coming through.

But even the roof won't prevent life's faults.

It will never be perfect.

But it still goes on,

Always moving, time never stops.

*Emma Crosbie*

Corrine Ciarney

# Pen

You use me to scribble down
your last minute history report on the school bus.
You use me to write a note on your hand,
to remind yourself to pick up your younger brother from school.

You furiously use me to write your heart-broken feelings
in your diary about the boyfriend that dumped you.
Or you can tearfully use me to write a letter to your Grandma,
telling her how much you miss and love her.

My emotions are the same as yours.
I feel whatever you want me to.
I mean so much more than e-mail or text.
My ink comes straight from the heart,
Like rivers straight from the ocean.

I'm very, very significant to your daily routine,
but I'm very, very undervalued.

Take me anywhere and everywhere.
I'll be ready.
I'll be ready to bring your thoughts and feelings
to life.

*Lisa Flaherty*

Katelynn Carroll

Ciaran Clifford

# Control the Media, Control the Mind
## With the Aid of Subliminal Messages

Open your eyes to the colours in front of you
It's an illusion
Of evolution,
A vision.
Can you dig that?
Listen to the deafening silence for once, twice, thrice
This life
It is heaven
Live, think it, know it, love it
These are the things that dreams are made of
Because the time to hesitate is through
The victor can only be you,
Or not, take your pick.
Live your life don't be an idiot
Cover your eyes;
Point to a place on the map
Find the way
Imagine
And go with the flow

*Matthew Manison*

# Control the Media, Control the Mind

A petrusion
An illusion
A subconscious thought
Devolved through the mind
Caged, left to rot.
A deep inner feeling
That needs to get out.
A puppet-master pulling your strings
Into a feeling of self-doubt.

*Michael Milarvie*

Rachael Holmes

# PART III

Paul Green

# My Little Brother

It's his monkey-like face
and stupid swagger.
It's his love for himself
and cocky manner.

How he steals my clothes
and uses my stuff.
How he's really just a wimp
when he acts all tough.

When his efforts to irritate
me succeed.
When I'm not in the mood,
it's not what I need.

Although...

As time goes by I hate to say,
we'll probably get along some day.
As we will live in different places,
we'll not be in each other's faces.

*Paul Green*

# My Little Sister

You may be smiles and hugs
when people are around.
You may be small and innocent
when company is found.
But behind this façade I know the truth,
you are the devil in disguise...

You always break my stuff.
You bully me at nights.
Whenever you don't get your way
you always pick a fight.
You always get your way.
I never get a say.
I hate the fact you're always right,
every single day.

My mum and dad both love you.
You're a blessing in their eyes.
I'm the only one who sees
through your evil disguise.
You're cocky: you're arrogant.
I hate the way you act.
I'm the victim in our house
and that is the truth.

*Ebony Lynch*

But… you help me when I'm sad.
You try to help me out.
You help me when I'm in a clinch,
and you never shout.
Despite all your childish acts
I do love you still.
You're my little sister
who I wouldn't want to kill.

*Jakob Taylor*

# Great Minds Think Alike

Laughing. Falling. Crying a river.
She's been there, right by my side forever.
We're like spaghetti and bolognaise,.
Never apart, crying over a broken heart.
We laugh and giggle and dance about.
We're the ones that you always hear shout.
Her style is so unique.
She has the confidence to take a sneaky peak.
We are forever acting daft and silly.
I couldn't live without my best friend, Lily.

*Marnie Smith*

Roxann Ingleby

# Best Friend

They say great minds think alike
And we say that sums us up.
We've been together since...
Since before I can remember -
Painting our faces in nursery,
Applying makeup as teens.
There's never been a day that you've not had me gaaaaaasping -
Gasping for air, in fits of laughter.
We're happy going out, dancing the night away -
Or curling up with a duvet, watching a movie.
Others may come and go
But we'll always be together -
Me and Marnie.

*Lily Morrison*

Paul Green

# Mi Amiga - Alidh O'Brien

Obsessively organised,
Pretty perfect,
Cat carer.
A star, to remember.
Eccentric eyelashes,
Repetitively right,
Pathetically paranoid.
She teases me, playfully.
Compulsively clean,
Selectively sensible,
Fabulously Funny.
Mi amiga, Ailidh.

*Megan Smith*

*Shannon Kerr*

# The Standoff

The smell of graphite and pencil shavings
As we finish our work,
Listening to music
Which isn't quite distracting enough,
From the growing silence between us.

You start a conversation that I won't continue,
Change the subject a few times.
I'll nod and brush you off
While you laugh at a joke we shared earlier.

Oh, we're as stubborn as each other,
You'll break me if you try hard enough -
Say something far too funny for me to ignore.
But I've dug my heels in now
And I won't reply until you apologise.

I'm not even sure what you've to say sorry for.
I can't remember.
It was something small
But it got to me,
As your blunt honesty often does.

Okay, now you're just irritating me,
Stop humming that song,
Telling that joke,
Replaying that conversation,
Stop trying to make me laugh,

*Cairan Clifford*

If you won't shut up, I'll do it for you,
And that's a promise.
But one I won't keep.

A heavy sigh and I surrender.
I can't win this war.
When you get like this, and won't give in,
I know you're really sorry.

I'll be honest.
You had me worried there,
I hate this too, this "argument" business,
Oh, we're as bad as each other.

*Katie Hughes*

Gillian Smyth

# My Granny June

My Granny June is full of smiles.
She gives great advice,
Shares stories that teach me,
Interest me.
She makes the greatest chips.

Sometimes,
When she walks into a room,
She'll pause at the doorway,
Purse her lips and look around,
And ask,
"Why did I come in here again?"
Then she'll leave the room
For a while,
Only to return with a triumphant cry of,
"Oh yes, that's why!"

When I ask her
How she is
She'll reply, "Fair to middling" or,
On a bad day,
"Fair to hellish".
I sometimes say these things as well.
I want to be just like her,
My Granny June.

*Rhiannon Fyfe*

# ACKNOWLEDGEMENTS

There are a number of people without whose diligence, encouragement and generosity this initiative would not have been possible.

I would like to thank Liz Lochhead for the way in which she gave of her time, and her willingness to share her expertise with the pupils. Monitoring the progress being made by 185 pupils within the English classes as they developed their poems was a major undertaking but one which she undertook with enthusiasm and energy. The pupils have benefitted greatly.

Special thanks also goes to Willie Rodger, who followed on, working with 150 pupils in the Art & Design classes as they sought to illustrate the poems written in English. He gave of his time generously and took a genuine interest in the work of each and every pupil.

As the poetry books have been produced, Vikki Reilly, of Birlinn Books and Susan Frize, of Milngavie Bookshop must also be thanked for their advice and support of the Business Education classes and Enterprise groups.

My personal thanks goes to the St Ninian's High School teachers who have been an inspiration to their classes and who have led their pupils through every stage of the learning process with a professionalism which has been greatly appreciated, to Caroline Harper and Lucy Prior, of the English department, to Maggi McNeill, of the Art & Design Department and to Joyce Gray and Moira Coleman, of the Business Education Department.

Thanks is also due to East Dunbartonshire Council which made it possible for both staff and pupils to work with the professionals and for the pupils to become published writers and artists themselves.

Above all, I would like to thank the young writers, artists and entrepreneurs who have taken this initiative to their hearts and made this book and its success a reality.

*Angela McEwan*
Editor

**Liz Lochhead** was born in Lanarkshire and was educated at Dalziel High School, Motherwell. Later she studied at Glasgow School of Art and graduated with a D.A. from the department of Drawing and Painting. She worked as an Art & Design teacher in various schools in the west of Scotland and England.

Her first collection of poetry was published in 1972. Several collections have been published since that time, the last one being *The Colour of Black and White*. During the 1980s she began writing plays which have been performed by the major Scottish theatre companies. Many of these, including *Mary Queen of Scots Got Her Head Chopped Off,* are in print.

Since 2005, Liz Lochhead has been Glasgow's Poet Laureate. She has been honoured by ten Scottish universities and various arts institutions.

**Willie Rodger** was born in Kirkintilloch and was educated at Lenzie Academy. He studied at Glasgow School of Art and graduated with a D.A. (Commercial and Graphic Design). Following a year as a graphic visualiser in advertising, he trained as an Art & Design teacher and taught in both Lenzie Academy and then as principal teacher in Clydebank High School.

Since 1954, work has been exhibited at both one-man and group exhibitions at major venues including the Open Eye, the Royal Scottish Academy, the Society of Scottish Arts. His work is exhibited at the Victoria & Albert Museum. He has also undertaken a range of design commissions. He collaborated with Liz Lochhead on her book, *The Colour of Black and White*, providing the lino-print illustrations for the book.

Willie Rodger is a fellow of the Royal Scottish Academy and in 1999 was made an honorary doctor of the University of Stirling.

# Joined Up Learning

As nine English classes in nine secondary schools worked together with poet, Liz Lochhead, the talk was about whether this word or that word was exactly right for the impression intended, whether this line length or that line length was the most effective. The pupils worked for six weeks (October - December 2009) developing their poems, changing them, explaining them and commenting on the 'work in progress' in each other's online 'jotter'. The internet was used to link the nine classes to each other and to Liz Lochhead, in discussion forums, in chat rooms and meeting together in live video conferences for tutorials on their work.

Liz, too, tried some of the writing tasks she set and commented - on their work and on her own. Some of the writers were in first year, some were in sixth year but they worked together to improve the writing, theirs and everyone else's... writing, reading, talking, listening, connected through a virtual classroom which included every secondary school in East Dunbartonshire and 185 pupils.

Six weeks on, each of the nine English classes met with an Art & Design class in their own school, and all eighteen classes linked together live online with both Liz Lochhead and Scotland's leading printmaker, Willie Rodger as Liz and Willie explained how he had illustrated her poetry collection, *The Colour of Black & White.* Each Art & Design class then worked with Willie Rodger between January and March 2010, developing, refining and refining their ideas for the prints which would illustrate each of the poems assigned to them by the English classes. The 150 art and design pupils learnt, first hand, the importance of their sketchbooks and how to cut images in lino.

Six weeks on, illustrated anthologies, featuring the poems and prints from each school, went into production. Business Education classes in seven of the schools and Enterprise groups in the other two met Vikki Reilly from publisher, Birlinn Books and Susan Frize, from independent bookseller, The Milngavie Bookshop in an online link to learn about and discuss together the marketing and selling of books.

Those 158 pupils involved in this third stage have the responsibility of selling the illustrated poetry anthologies - of which this book is one - to their own customers, as well as to independent bookshops and major booksellers. They are running book events in their schools and creating an online presence.

As with the English classes and the Art & Design classes, Business Education classes and Enterprise groups are linked together online, sharing ideas and acting as nine Social Enterprises, with net profits from the sale of each book going to a range of charities chosen by the pupils taking part in each school.

St Ninian's High School has chosen to support the Scottish Catholic International Aid Fund (SCIAF).

'Joined Up Learning' is a unique initiative in which pupils from different year groups and from different departments within each school have not only worked together but also with English or Art & Design or Business Education classes and Enterprise groups from every other secondary school in their local authority.

Staff in each school have worked together with their subject colleagues in the other schools and with teachers from other departments in their own school, using internet technology to enhance teaching and learning.

*English, Art & Design, Business Education,*
*Enterprise, Literacy, Numeracy, Citizenship, ICT*

*Curriculum for Excellence in Action*

# Joined Up Learning Series

*'The relationship between writing and drawing is immediate and ancient, visible at first glance to the page, but also rising from a long tradition of complementary work between poets and writers and artists of all kinds: the connection is clear if you think about what words like image, line, form and rhythm really mean. All the work in this series of books is galvanized by this connection. Each singular example is a kind of revelation of unsuspected insight, an illumination. And at its best, when this kind of illumination gives you something you really could not have predicted before, you take with you something worth keeping in mind. The creative potential of young people is our richest resource for the future. These books show what good provision can bring. Beyond the storms and droughts, there is evidence here of good weather ahead.'*

Professor Alan Riach, Chair of Scottish literature, Glasgow University

*'I very much enjoyed reading these collections. I was struck by the emotional honesty of the writers, as well as the beautifully crafted language and the energy and joy they conveyed. The wonderful illustrations worked beautifully with the text, making these books a real delight.'*

Anne Donovan, author of *Buddha Da*

*'What wonderful collections! Each one engages head, heart and eye. The black and white illustrations capture subject and mood in strikingly original forms.'*

Christine Findlay, author of *The Colonel's Collection*

*'These books represent a fertile collaboration between pupils, teachers, and two very special mentors in the disciplines of art and literature: an alliance through which ideas and inspiration have passed as effortlessly as light through glass.*

*And if the purpose of education is to draw out rather than to put in, then this glorious association has achieved its aim. With inspiration from the poet and playwright, Liz Lochhead and the visual artist Willie Rodger, creative juices have been set flowing. The happy coalition of two separate art forms has amplified the original stimulus, increased its poignancy, and, with no disjunction between style and substance, released the expressive potential that often lies hidden within the ordinary and the everyday.*

*Moods and feelings have been given a palpable form that transcends visual or emotional origins creating words and images that are acceptable metaphors for life. The lesson has been learned: art confirms the narratives that make sense of our lives. In reflecting their own thoughts and feelings each of these young artists and writers has wheedled from the coarse material of life some fundamental truths about human existence. And by giving permanence to transitory experience they have exposed both a dramatic intensity and a tender beauty in the sincerity of their intentions.'*

Anne Ellis, art historian, broadcaster,
and former curator of The Hill House

"Learning is being able to see the relationship between things."
Jean Renoir

# THE JOINED UP LEARNING SERIES

*From the Den of the Bear*  ... Bearsden Academy

*Animals, Abstracts & Allsorts*
  ... Bishopbriggs Academy

*Write Out of Our Heads*  ... Boclair Academy

*Colour in Shadows*  ... Douglas Academy

*A Picture Speaks a Thousand Words*
  ... Kirkintilloch High School

*Cutting Verse*  ... Lenzie Academy

*Time Flies...*  ... Merkland School

*Fruitful Thoughts of Adolescents*
  ... St Ninian's High School

*Picture Perfect Poems*  ... Turnbull High School

http://www.mediamatters.co.uk/JoinedUpLearning/

Lightning Source UK Ltd.
Milton Keynes UK
26 May 2010

154752UK00001B/1/P